Environmental Crime Scene Processing

A book by

Michael W. Weissberg

WHITE MOUNTAIN PUBLISHING CO.

MIAMI, FLORIDA

2011

WHITE MOUNTAIN PUBLISHING CO.
MIAMI, FLORIDA

First edition

Library of Congress Cataloging-in-Publication Data

Weissberg, Michael.

Environmental Crime Scene Processing by Michael Weissberg – 1st ed.

Library of Congress Control Number (LCCN):
PCN 2011928144

ISBN-10 0983486646
ISBN-13 9780983486640

10 9 8 7 6 5 4 3 2 1

Book design by Michael Weissberg

Printed in the United States of America

Also by Michael Weissberg

Honor, Glory, Respect:
Conducting Police Funerals

Coming Soon from White Mountain
Publishing Company:

What Every Cop Must Know:
Tactical Preparation for the Worst Day
of Your Life

Concealed Weapons
Carry For Cops

Acknowledgements

For my son Dean Bennett Bacon Weissberg, and for Erika: thanks for being my wife.

About the Author
Michael W. Weissberg

Michael Weissberg began his career as an educator in 1988. A graduate of the University of Miami, Weissberg holds Master's degrees in Education, Criminal Justice, and Psychology from Nova Southeastern University, Florida International University, and Northcentral University, as well as a Graduate Certificate in Criminal Justice Administration and Policy Making and Industrial Organizational Psychology with a focus on Law Enforcement Management.

Professor Weissberg has taught on the undergraduate level at Miami Dade College, St. Thomas University, and Florida International University, and graduate school at Nova Southeastern University; he was Director of Crime Scene Programs at Miami Dade College and served as a

Crime Scene Investigator and instructor, and started a crime scene unit, designed the crime lab, and did budgeting, ordering, and training for his department.

Sgt. Weissberg has served as a Police Officer, Administrative Officer, Crime Scene Investigator, Police Detective, and a Police Sergeant, and Acting Lieutenant.

Dedication

Detective Mike Byrd was assigned to the Miami-Dade Police Department Crime Scene Section, where he spent the majority of his 19-year law enforcement career.

Mike was a certified police standards instructor for the states of Florida and Arkansas. He taught for the Miami-Dade Training Bureau, the Miami-Dade County Medical Examiner Department and many Florida police departments.

Michael developed and instructed the *"Crime Scene Evaluation and Latent Fingerprint Recovery"* class that has been referred to as the "Field Training Officer's" crime scene class.

Mike wrote more than 30 articles for the Florida Division of the International Association for the Identification (FDIAI) and the IAI and was awarded the "Good of the Association Award" in 2002 for his innovative identification methodology and techniques. In 2001, he published a professional handbook entitled *"Crime Scene Evidence: A Guide to the Recovery and Collection of Physical Evidence,"* a hands-on manual used nationally by crime scene investigation units.

Mike performed the tough detail-oriented forensic work at many major crime scenes and disasters over his career. He gathered, processed, and identified the DNA evidence to convict the Tamiami Strangler in 1994, and after gathering evidence at the Valuejet crash, he wrote an article on organization and leadership for disaster response: *Disaster Management - Lost Innocents.*

Mike Byrd died of cancer. Even though Mike was a consummate professional, in the early days of crime scene, the carcinogenic effects of fingerprint powder were unknown, and may have contributed to his death.

The author learned much of his early crime scene information from Mike Byrd's classes.

In memory of
Detective Mike Byrd
Miami Dade Police Department
19 Year Veteran

To honor fallen Police Officers:

The National Law Enforcement Officers Memorial is the nation's monument to law enforcement officers who have died in the line of duty. Please donate.

If you would like to contribute by phone, please call 202-737-3400.

If you would like to contribute by Mail, please write:

NLEOMF
901 E Street NW, Suite 100
Washington, DC 20004-2025
info@nleomf.org

The Police Officer's Assistance Trust was founded in 1989 as a nonprofit support organization for the law enforcement community of Miami-Dade County, Florida. To make a donation in honor of

Detective Mike Byrd
Miami Dade Police Department

Contact:
Police Officer's Assistance Trust
1030 NW 111 Avenue,
Miami, Florida 33172
305.594.6662
Email: poatoffice@msn.com

A PORTION OF THE SALE OF THIS BOOK WILL BE DONATED TO POAT FOR THE FAMILIES OF OFFICRS KILLED IN LINE OF DUTY IN MIAMI-DADE COUNTY, FLORIDA.

Introduction

You will read things here that may be unpopular, may make you angry, and may save your life. Environmental crime scenes are especially dangerous to the world we live in. The proper processing and documentation of these scenes is important.

This book is for you; not because I know so much, because I don't. It's because we know so little, are our own worst enemies, and because we forget so much. As I said in my last book: The best we can do, is the least we can do.

Non soleus, (Never alone)

The Author

Introduction to Environmental Crime Scenes

This type of crime is not only a danger to the land, water, air, but to animals, and people, especially the police officer or CSI.

The First Responder has the ability to evaluate and observe evidence that may be fleeting (may evaporate rapidly) and photo document or document by notes or sketches. Approach from upwind with caution!

Block off traffic if necessary. Determine if chemical evidence is changing or evaporating. The investigator should document color changes, reactions, degradation, expansion, or other changes in the evidence. A change in temperature, moisture, wind direction, or the addition of rain can affect evidence.

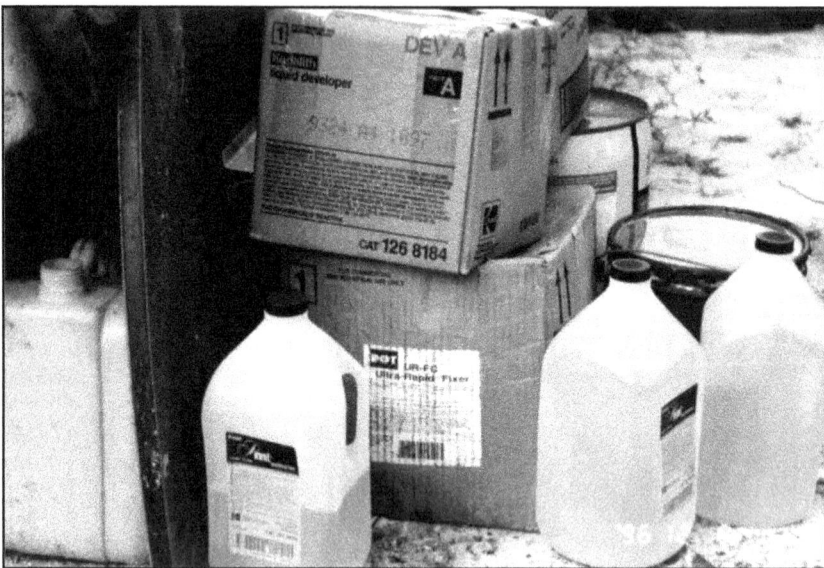

Note the shape of the jugs is changing.

Write down who was on the scene upon your arrival. Establish the basic facts. Keep suspects and witnesses separate if possible.

Establish the Locard Log. Establish the perimeter with crime scene tape.

The Locard Log is named for the Locard Exchange Principle. Everyone Signs in with their name, rank, and purpose.

Everyone who enters a scene takes material away with them, and brings material in with them. This is called the "The Locard Exchange Principle".

The Locard Exchange Principle developed by Edmond Locard at the University of Lyon in 1910. The principle says that anyone who enters a scene brings things to the scene and takes things away from the scene.

On a major scene where an unlawful homicide has been committed or the victim is likely to die, the responding officer should start a Locard Log.

The investigation of environmental crime involves the same

skills as used in traditional crimes, but with a twist. This can be as simple as collecting a water sample in a vial or as involved as two weeks of processing a HAZMAT scene outdoors, in the middle of a swamp in august during the mosquito mating season, such as in the "Valujet" crash in Miami, Florida.

Special hazards include radioactive materials, acutely hazardous chemicals, and pressurized containers.

Harris v. US

Nearly every crime lab in the country has this quote from Harris v. United States, 331 U.S. 145 (1947) posted somewhere in the lab:

"Wherever he steps, whatever he touches, whatever he leaves, even unconsciously, will serve as a silent witness against him.

Not only his fingerprints or his footprints, but his hair, the fibers from his clothes, the glass he breaks, the tool mark he leaves, the paint he scratches, the blood or semen he deposits or collects, all of these will bear mute witness against him.

This is evidence that does not forget. It is not confused by the excitement of the moment. It is not absent because human witnesses are. It is factual evidence.

Physical evidence cannot be wrong; it cannot perjure itself; it cannot be wholly absent. Only its interpretation can err. Only human failure to find it, study it and understand it can diminish its value."

Safeguarding Evidence

You must safeguard evidence; once an item of evidence has been altered or moved, it is impossible to restore it to its original position or condition. Establish a PIO or media area.

Instruct witnesses not to discuss events. Do not discuss crime with witnesses, suspects, victims, or bystanders.

- listen to what is being said.
- protect evidence.
- record changes in conditions

Infinite Monkey Theorem

The infinite monkey theorem states that a monkey hitting keys at random on a typewriter keyboard for an infinite amount of time will almost surely type a given text, such as the complete works of William Shakespeare.

These statements can be traced back to Aristotle's *On Generation and Corruption* and Cicero's *De natura deorum*, through Blaise Pascal and Jonathan Swift, and finally to modern statements with their iconic typewriters; or alternately, according to Scott Adams, you get a room full of dead monkeys.

The Alternate Hypothesis (Ha) is that a monkey hitting keys at random on a typewriter keyboard for an infinite amount of time will almost surely type a given text, such as the complete works of William Shakespeare; the Null Hypothesis (Ho) is that a monkey hitting keys at random on a typewriter keyboard for an infinite amount of time will *not* type a given text, such as the complete works of William Shakespeare.

$\mu_1 \neq \mu_2$ means that one may reject the null (Ho). $\mu_1 = \mu_2$ conclusion: means that one may fail to reject the null (Ho).

Using these hypotheses, and a bit of imagination, you can conclude that a CSI dusting things at a crime scene at random for an infinite amount of time will almost surely result in the collection of fingerprints. Time, effort, and money (resources) are factors, so if one had an unlimited supply of each, one could find fingerprints on any scene.

The reality is, that you will not have unlimited time, effort, and money, so there are scenes that will yield nothing useful; the bosses and the victims will just have to deal with that.

The Effects of TV
on the Bosses

I once had a chief of police ask me why it took twenty-one months to get DNA evidence back from the lab, when they could get it on *CSI Miami* in twenty minutes. I was astounded; my flabber was gasted. How could a man be chief of police and not know the difference between television and reality?

CSI Miami and shows like it have done more for crime scene units and more to hurt crime scene units than anything in recent memory. No money was allotted to CSI until these shows; no training dollars were available.

A city manager once asked "don't you just throw some dust around and leave? My entire profession could be replaced by Tinkerbell.

Suddenly there was money for gadgetry. I once saw my partner turned down because she wanted a pocket knife. She told me she didn't owned one, and had never owned one, but wanted one for cutting finger print tape. I put in the budget for a "crime scene lifting media bifurcation device. It soared through, since no one knew what I was talking about, and no one wanted to admit that. I purchased the knife, which she carries to this day.

Then there was the time that a sergeant informed me she was the new supervisor for my unit. This was the fifth sergeant I had to "break in" in about five years. She told me: "tell me what it is that you do here so I can tell you if you are doing it right". The words just hung there and smelled like bad cheese. We both laughed. I got a good evaluation.

Occam's Razor

Occam's Razor (Ockham's Razor) or in Latin, *lex parsimoniae*, or the law of parsimony (succinctness), is a principle that generally recommends selecting the competing hypothesis that makes the fewest new assumptions, when the hypotheses are equal in other respects. In other words, if you see horseshoe prints, look for a horse, before you look for a zebra; the simplest explanation is more often the correct one. This philosophy is one of several demonstrated in the popular medical adage *"when you are in Texas and you hear hoofbeats, think horses, not zebras."*

William of Ockham (c. 1285–1349) is remembered as an influential logician rests chiefly on the maxim attributed to him and known as Ockham's razor. The term razor (the

German *Ockhams Messer* translates to *Occam's knife*) refers to distinguishing between two theories either by "shaving away" unnecessary assumptions or cutting apart two similar theories.

In physics, parsimony was an important heuristic in the formulation of special relativity by Albert Einstein. The principle is most often expressed as e*ntia non sunt multiplicanda praeter necessitatem,* or *entities should not be multiplied beyond necessity*, but this sentence was written by later authors and is not found in Ockham's surviving writings.

This also applies to *non est ponenda pluritas sine necessitate,* which translates into English as *"pluralities ought not be posited without necessity"*. It has inspired numerous expressions including *parsimony of postulates*, the *principle of simplicity*, and *the KISS principle (Keep It Simple, Stupid)*.

Occam's Razor is normally stated as *"of two equivalent theories or explanations, all other things being equal, the simpler one is to be preferred.*" Sir Isaac Newton rephrased it as "*we are to admit no more causes of natural things than such as are both true and sufficient to explain their appearances*".

This means that regardless of what you see on television or in the movies, do not get bogged down with complicated, unlikely theories necessitating unwieldy equipment, time consuming processes, or expensive chemicals, when a simplistic approach may be best.

Buridan's Ass

Buridan's Ass is an illustration of a paradox in philosophy in the conception of free will. It refers to a hypothetical situation wherein an ass is placed precisely midway between a stack of hay and a pail of water. Since the paradox assumes the ass will always go to whichever is closer, it will die of both hunger and thirst since it cannot make any rational decision to choose one over the other.

The paradox is named after the 14th century French philosopher Jean Buridan, whose philosophy of moral determinism it satirizes.

The song *Freedom of Choice* by the American band Devo contains lyrics which refer to a dog who runs in circles when confronted with a choice of two bones, eventually dropping dead.

This paradox exists when a CSI has to decide between swabbing a greasy print for DNA or processing it for dactyloscopic analysis, either of which will render the other process impossible.

Two common types of fingerprint sources submitted for DNA analysis are from sweaty or bloody latent fingerprints. The DNA provided through a sweaty handprint is from cells sloughed off during contact with a surface.

In a bloody fingerprint, the DNA comes from the white blood cells. In the case of bloody fingerprints, however, it is important to be aware that the primary source of DNA being obtained is from the blood source and not from any sloughed-off cells of the individual who left the fingerprint. The amount of the sample is important in determining whether there is sufficient DNA to obtain a profile.

Due to the large number of white blood cells, blood has a high concentration of DNA; therefore, an area the size of the head of a pin is usually sufficient to obtain a profile. Priority should first be given to the lifting and photographing of the fingerprint. Areas that are deemed not to be of evidentiary value by the latent print examiner can then be swabbed and transferred to the forensic-biology section of the crime lab for DNA analysis.

The dual use of both fingerprint and DNA identification technologies provides the investigator with two means of identifying an unknown subject. (see also *Second Chance: Guidelines on Conducting DNA Analysis of Latent Prints* in Evidence Technology Magazine Volume:1 Issue:2 Dated: July-August 2003 Pages: 33 to 35 by Michael W. Weissberg and Amy M. Ruggles).

Do not confuse this with a Hobson's choice, a free choice in which only one option is offered. As a person may refuse to take that option, the choice is therefore between taking the option or not; *take it or leave it.*

The phrase is said to originate with Thomas Hobson (1544–1631), a livery stable owner in Cambridge, England. To rotate the use of his horses, he offered customers the choice of either taking the horse in the stall nearest the door or taking none at all.

Being between Scylla and Charybdis is an idiom deriving from Greek mythology. Several other idioms, such as *on the horns of a dilemma* and *between the devil and the deep blue sea* express the same meaning of *having to choose between two evils*.

Do not confuse this with a Morton's Fork, a choice between two equally unpleasant alternatives (in other words, a dilemma), or two lines of reasoning that lead to the same unpleasant conclusion. It is analogous to the expression *between a rock and a hard place*, or, as those in the Spanish- and Portuguese-speaking world say, b*etween a sword and the wall*. This is the opposite of the Buridan's Ass.

The expression originates from a policy of tax collection devised by John Morton, Lord Chancellor of England in 1487, under the rule of Henry VII. His approach was that if the subject lived in luxury and had clearly spent a lot of money on himself, he obviously had sufficient income to spare for the king.

Alternatively, if the subject lived frugally, and showed no sign of being wealthy, he must have substantial savings and could therefore afford to give it to the king. These arguments were the two prongs of the fork and regardless of whether the subject was rich or poor, he did not have a favorable choice.

Sometimes, you will lose. Sometimes you will try something new and destroy what evidence you did have. If you do not try new procedures, or invent procedures, or try established procedures that are unfamiliar to you, then you will not grow as a CSI.

A Word About
The Media

In a high profile case, such as a murder, do not discuss the case over the radio or cell phone, as it will be monitored by the media.

Have an incident commander, supervisor, and PIO respond to major scenes. Cordon off an area for media. Remember, it is easy to move a perimeter in, but harder to move one back. You may need several layers of scene tape for spectators, media, and officers.

Any media violating scene tape and entering the scene should be restrained, warned, and if necessary, arrested.

Call-Outs

Call out the Investigators, CSI's, Detectives, and supervisors as SOPs' dictate.

Other call outs may include:

- HAZMAT
- FBI
- DEA
- BATF
- Fire Marshall

Securing the Scene

First, Approach from upwind. Secure the scene. This is most important. Your primary objective is to go home at end of shift. Make sure the violator is no longer on the scene.

- Your first responsibility is to yourself.

- Your second responsibility is to your family.

- Your third responsibility is to your squad.

- Your fourth responsibility is to your department.

- Your fifth responsibility is to your city or county.

- Your next responsibility is to protect and to serve the public.

Do Not Taste Anything on a Scene!

Regardless of what you see on television, do not taste anything on a scene! Many shows and movies, including my favorite, *Running Scared* with Gregory Hines and Billy Crystal, depict cops tasting cocaine to see if it is real.

"THOSE WHO TASTE AND WONDER "WHY" ARE THE ONES WHO SURELY DIE."

Do Not Smell Anything on a Scene!

Regardless of what you see on television, do not smell anything on a scene! The reason you can smell things is that they are on your tongue and in your sinuses, and your mucous membranes.

"THOSE WHO WISH TO TAKE A SNIFF, ARE THE ONES WHO END UP STIFF."

One mistake can be
Immediately fatal!

Medical Considerations as a First Responder

Assist any persons needing medical attention. Use the Acronym "Sludge" to determine if there is a HAZMAT situation.

"SLUDGE"

SALIVATE
LACRYMATE
URINATE
DEFICATE
GASTROINTESTINAL DISTRESS
EMESIS

If you see people with these signs and symptoms, know that you may need self contained breathing apparatus due to gas, acid, or other HAZMAT situations.

Bloodborne pathogens are a real consideration. HIV (Human Immunodeficiency Virus) symptoms may not show up for years, and eventually develops into AIDS (Acquired Immune Deficiency Syndrome). Aids related illnesses include cancer, neurological problems, infections, and pneumonia.

HBV (Hepatitis B Virus) results in an inflammation of the liver. Untreated, it leads to liver damage, cirrhosis, and death.

Hepatitis and HIV can be transmitted through blood, or any body fluid.

- Follow policy
- Report contamination
- Use PPE and universal precautions

After Giving Medical Help

Preserve the crime scene. Your next step is to make sure evidence remains uncontaminated. Cordon off the area with scene tape. Make the scene as big as you need to, then double the scene. If there are several scenes, treat them as separate scenes.

Dealing With Family Members

Family members or property owners should not be allowed on a crime scene. Restrain hysterical or overwrought family carefully, and with kindness.

When There Is A Body On A Scene

If there is a body on the scene, and the person is believed to be dead, only one fire rescue person should enter the scene, and without a stretcher.

If the person is obviously dead (postmortem lividity or livor mortis, rigor mortis, algor mortis, decapitation, or decomposition) then no fire rescue should enter the scene.

If fire rescue determines that the person is alive, no life-saving efforts should be obstructed by police. Rescue personnel should be cautioned to disturb the scene as little as possible.

Scene Search

A crime scene search is a planned, coordinated, and legal search by law enforcement officers or crime scene investigators to locate physical evidence. There is only one chance to search the scene properly.

There are 3 types of searches commonly used:

The strip or line search, is often used for trying to locate missing persons with large number of searchers:

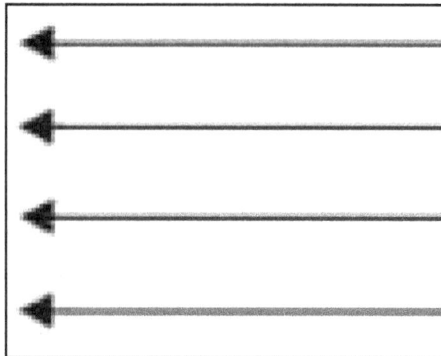

The grid search is the most time consuming. This is used for searching for evidence, as in the Valujet Crash:

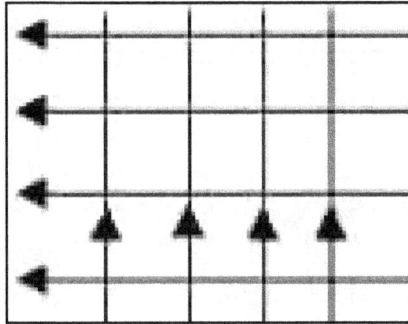

The spiral search is often used to canvass an area:

Crime Scene

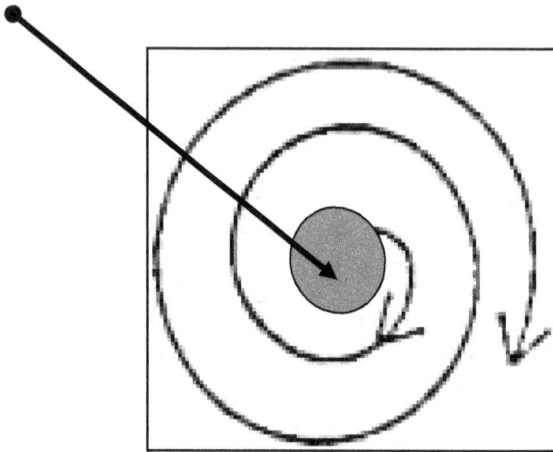

First, conduct a cautious search of visible areas, avoiding evidence loss or contamination. Then, after a cautious search, conduct a vigorous search of concealed areas. Taking copious notes, making sketches, and taking photographs are all essential to documenting the scene.

Notes should include the date, time, location, case number, case identifier (type of case, e.g., homicide, rape), weather, lighting conditions, personnel present and their assignments, and the condition and position of the evidence.

A crime scene template may be used to sketch scenes. If the sketch is not to scale, it should be labeled "not to scale". A crime scene sketching program may be used for better sketches.

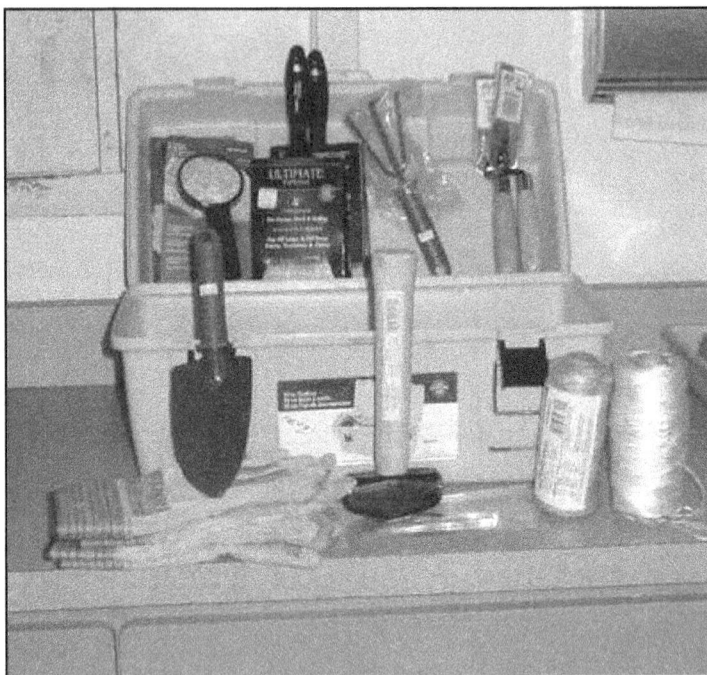

Search Kit:
Trowel, gloves, string, hammer, claw,
magnifying glass, gloves, brushes.
Photographed at the Miami Dade
County Medical Examiner's Office.

Search Kit:
Compass, plumb bob, level, measuring
tape, photo scale, calipers, orange
marking tape, nails. Photographed at
the Miami Dade County Medical
Examiner's Office.

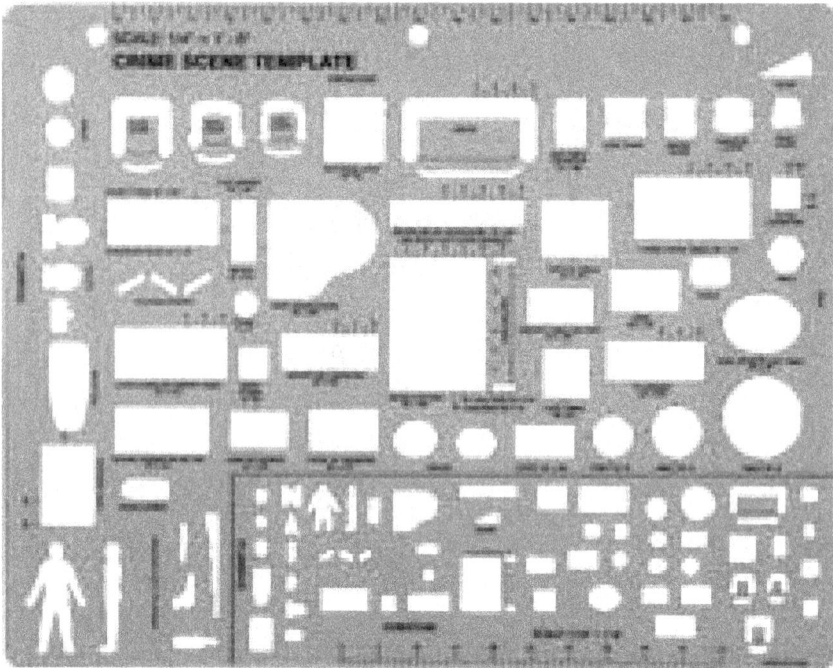

A Crime Scene Template for sketching.

The best search options are typically the most difficult and time-consuming. Physical evidence cannot be over documented. There is only one chance to search the scene properly.

The person in charge is responsible for scene security, administrative log, preliminary survey, narrative description, problem resolution, and final decision making.

The Sketch Preparer completes the sketch and log. The Evidence Recorder is responsible for acting as the evidence custodian and log. The Photographer is responsible for the photography and photo log.

Release the crime scene after the final survey.

▶ Crime scene release documentation should include the time and date of release, to whom released, and by whom released.

▶ Ensure that the evidence is collected according to legal requirements, documented, and marked for identification.

▶ Consider the need for specialists such as a blood-pattern analyst or a medical examiner to observe the scene before it is released.

▶ Once the scene has been released, reentry may require a warrant.

▶ The scene should be released only when all personnel are satisfied that the scene was searched correctly and completely.

▶ Only the person in charge should release the scene.

▶ Once the scene is released, a warrant may be necessary to get back in. Don't rush to release the scene, even when administrators or owners complain.

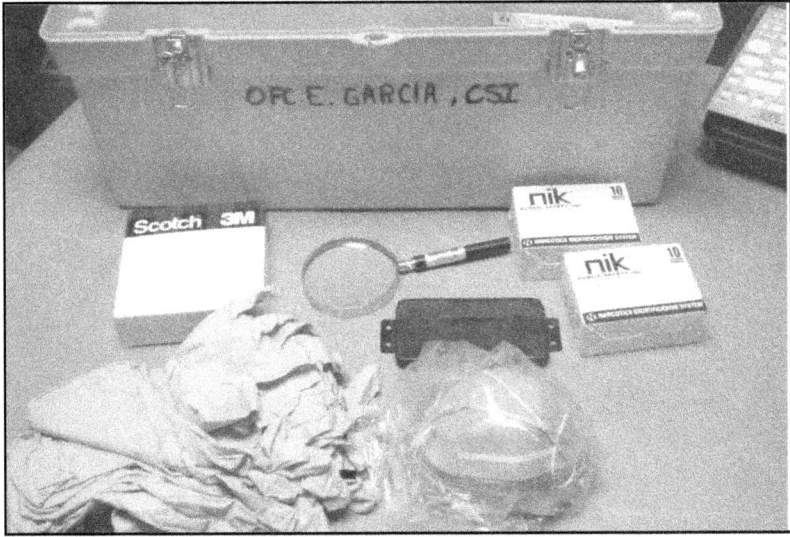

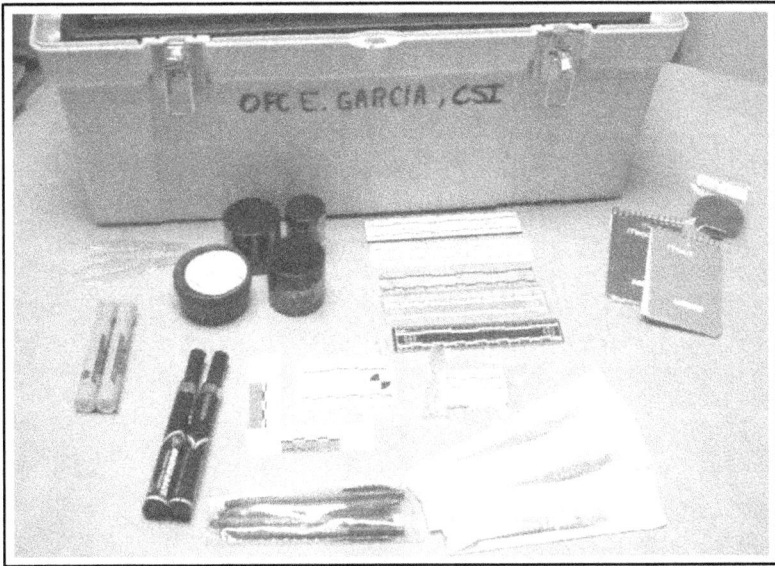

A good CSI kit can be assembled for less money than a preassembled kit from a catalog.

CSI Tools

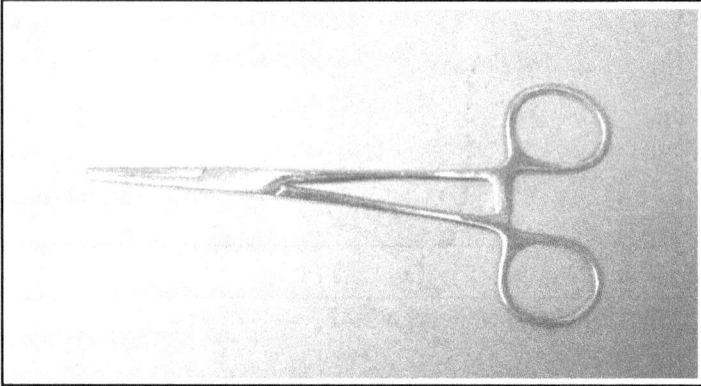

Forceps can be had for a few dollars, allow you to pick up items without contaminating them, and make you look more professional on a scene.

Everyone expects to see it, so why not give them what they want? The magnifier also helps the CSI to see the makeup of the print. Very greasy prints will smear, and should not be used with powder. MoS2 works better.

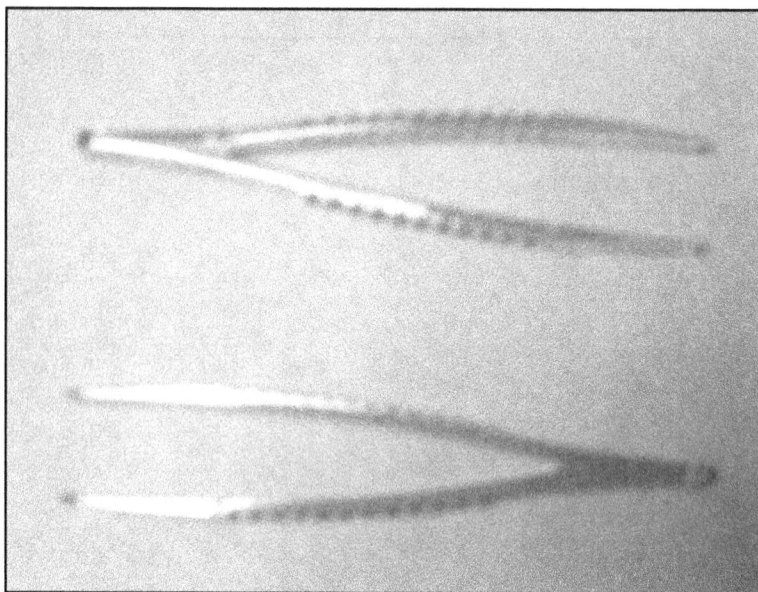

*Disposable plastic tweezers should be
used to pick up contaminated items.*

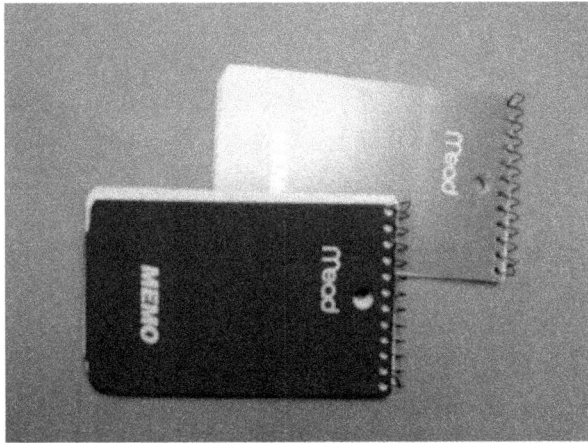

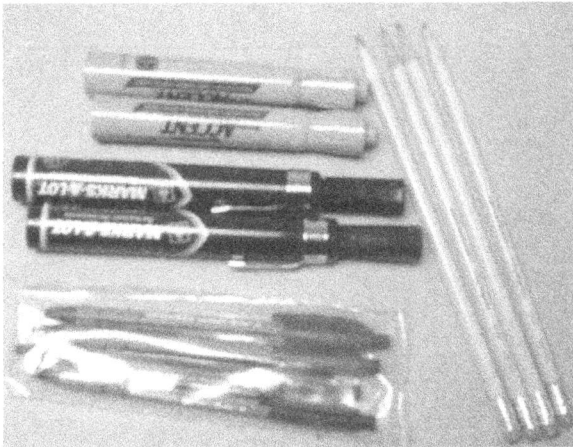

Throw a few extra memo books, pens, pencils, and markers in a plastic bag, or better yet, seal them in plastic. Running out is worse than having too many.

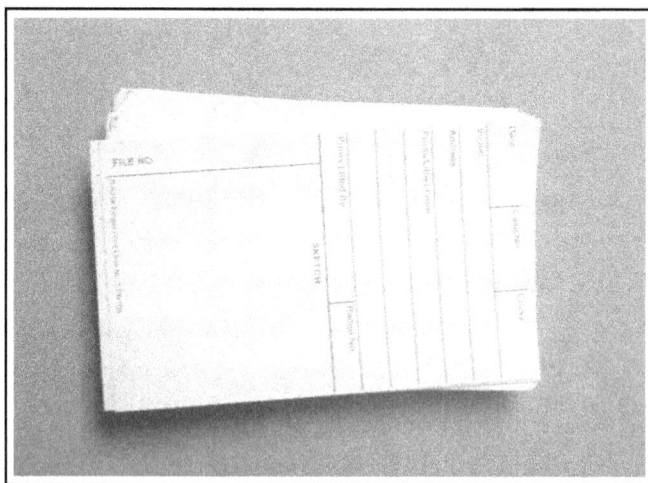

The tools of the trade; remember, the brushes, wands, and dust are to be considered contaminated and single-use on a hazardous crime scene.

Dead Animals on a Scene

The investigator should impound entire animals for necropsy and sampling. Water samples, sediment samples, soil samples, and plant samples all have evidentiary value.

The sampling order should be from the most contaminated or most dangerous to least contaminated or least dangerous.

Photography

Establishing shots should be made of the overall scene. Photo cards should contain the case number, name and initial of officer collecting, date, and time.

Close-up photos should be made of everything relevant before and after photos should be made of any area that a fingerprint is to be collected. 1:1 photos should be made of any evidence collected. Photos should include odontological scale or crime scene ruler.

"5-S" method

Sight - does the air, soil, water, or vegetation look different? Is the soil lighter or darker than normal?

Sound - is the area mysteriously quiet, with an absence of bird, animal, or insect sounds normally present?

Smell – is there a strong, bitter, sweet, or unusual odor present?

Secretive – is there something suspicious going on, like midnight construction?

Shift – does a company employee report that legal activities have changed or shifted to a new or illegal procedure?

Significant Environmental Harm

"Significant Environmental Harm" is identifiable harm to human health or environment by discharge, release, or emission, the threat of identifiable harm to human health or environment by discharge, release, or emission, the failure to report Identifiable harm to human health or environment by discharge, release, or emission, or the illegal conduct which represents non-compliance within the regulated community.

That is a mouthful by any standard. Using the term "Significant Environmental Harm" on an arrest form is like using the magic words. This is the term the judge and the jury will remember, and must be attached to the offender by the testimony.

Four Primary
Evidence Categories

There are four primary evidence categories:

- Chemical evidence: (xylene, paint, toluene, paint stripper, oil)

- Biological evidence: (medical waste, dead animals, plants, fish & birds)

- Physical evidence: (prints, tool marks, papers, tire impressions, stain patterns)

- Testimonial evidence: ("I saw them dump this here").

All four categories are equally important.

Accessing Containers For Samples

Accessing containers for samples can be hazardous. Consider container integrity, chemical reactivity, stability, sensitivity, and shelf life when making decisions. Chemicals can be carcinogenic, mutinagenic, or teratagenic. Exposure can cause sickness, cancer, mutation, or death.

- Carcinogenic – causes cancer

- Mutinogenic – causes mutations

- Teratogenic – causes birth defects

Universal Precautions

Again, the ultimate responsibility is to yourself. Do not risk contaminating yourself with blood or body fluids without protection.

Shoe covers, rubber gloves, masks, respirators, goggles, and gowns should be available for workers who require them.

The International Association for Identification makes safety recommendations that should be followed.

Particulate matter respirators should be used on scenes where decomposition or disease may be present.

Never place a cap on a needle or place a needle in a container. Place the container over the needle or the cap over the needle. Needle sticks can be deadly.

Hepatitis and Aids can kill. Do not risk contamination.

Some other equipment you should have is:

- Latex gloves

- Tyvek shoe covers

- Tyvek or Kleenguard suits

- Mask / respirator

- Goggles

- Red biohazard waste bags

- Level B SCBA

No eating, drinking, smoking, applying makeup should be done before decontamination. A 10% bleach or microbial soap for cleanup is recommended. Do not take contaminated clothing home to clean or sanitize. Remember pets and children live on the floor, and put everything in their mouths. Do not track these dangerous chemicals or solids into your home.

The environmental crime scene can be one of the most dangerous and most important crime scenes that you can work.

Regardless if you are a patrol officer, a detective, or a crime scene investigator, there are specialists in every community, so never try to do more than you are competent to do. The scene can be deadly to everyone in the area.

Latent Prints

Dactyloscopy is The Science of fingerprinting. A fingerprint is an individual characteristic. No two fingerprints have ever been found to have the same ridge characteristics. Skin cells nearest to the surface that make up the outer portion of the skin are called the epidermis.

Minutae are the ridge characteristics that make up a fingerprint. Minutae points give the individuality to the ridges. These include dot, bifurcation, trifurcation, enclosure, bridge, ending, and spur.

A fingerprint will remain unchanged during a person's lifetime, unless changed through a burn, cut, scar, or other means. A fingerprint has general ridge patterns that permit it to be systematically classified. Classification is done in three main types: loops, whorls, and arches.

AFIS is the Automated Fingerprint Identification System. AFIS converts image of print into digital minutae. An AFIS search can conduct an operation in minutes, which previously would have taken 50 years, working 24 hours a day, seven days a week.

A fingerprint is made up of materials from the eccrine glands, sebaceous glands, and apocrine glands.

The eccrine glands secrete inorganics: chlorides, metal ions, ammonia, sulfates, and phosphates; they also secrete organics: amino acids, urea, lactic acid, choline, uric acid, creatinine, and sugars.

The sebaceous glands secrete inorganics, such as fatty acids, glycerides, alcohol, and hydrocarbons.

The apocrine glands secrete inorganics, such as sodium, potassium, and iron, and organics, such as proteins, carbohydrates, and cholesterol.

In order to recover a print, you must choose the right process!

Processes are either physical or chemical. Here are some examples:

- Physical – fingerprint dust is attracted to moisture. Fingerprint dust is the most common way to recover prints. On the back of the fingerprint card, put the following:

    1. Case Number

    2. Case Reference

    3. Name

    4. Id #

    5. Sketch

- Physical – magnetic fingerprint dust is attracted to moisture.

- Physical - superglue is attracted to moisture. Fumes react and produce hard, visible impressions, turning them to plastic which can be dusted and lifted more than once.

- Chemical - Ninhydrin identifies amino acids.

- Chemical - silver nitrate identifies chlorides.

- Chemical – Sudan black identifies lipids and fats.

- Chemical – iodine identifies lipids and fats.

- Chemical – Amido black identifies proteins.

- Chemical – SPR / MOS2 identifies lipids and fats.

Elimination Prints

Elimination prints can be used to eliminate a subject, or can be used to compare to a set of prints lifted from a crime scene to be used as a standard.

If there is a person that is supposed to be there, a manager or an employee, the elimination prints can be used to take their prints out of a selection of lifted prints, so that the latent examiner doesn't spend time trying to identify prints.

The prints of a known person can be taken using an ink slab or Porelon pad. Both rolled and plain impressions should be taken. Palm prints, and the "karate chop" or writer's palm should also be taken.

A suspect can be asked to give elimination prints to eliminate him or her as a suspect, and then have the prints compared to the latents that were lifted. At any time, a suspect can be asked for a buccal cheek swab or a set of prints. If the subject wants to give them, then they are ok to take.

If later, something is suppressed, it may hurt the case, but it is better to have something and have it suppressed later, then try to get a warrant to force a set of prints, blood, or a buccal swab. These may be considered types of searches.

Consent is the most powerful search, followed by a search warrant, inventory search, search incident to arrest, and finally probable cause. If someone is voluntarily allowing you to search his house, car, person, or property, have a witness, or better yet, a signed permission form from the owner of the property or the person to be searched.

Good arrests can be made from prints taken as "eliminations" which later tie a person to a crime scene.

A Porelon Pad and a thumbprint pad for taking eliminations.

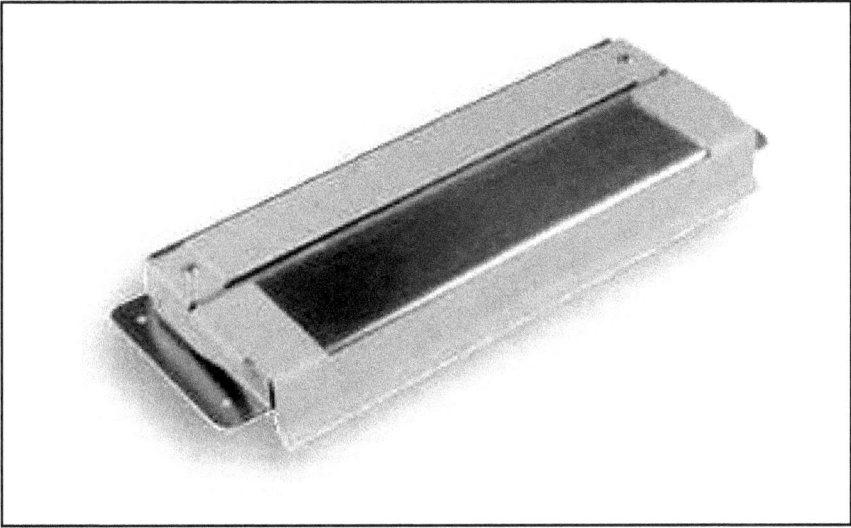

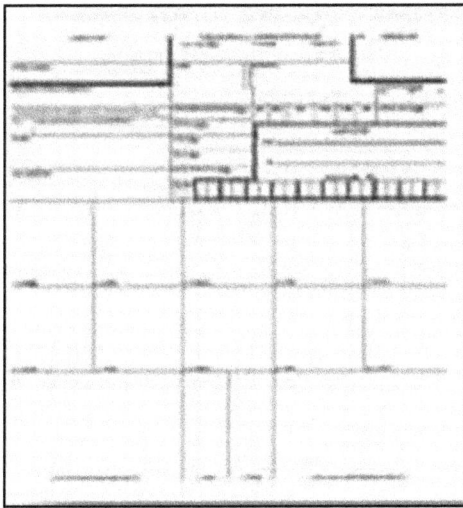

A 10 Print card holder and the card it uses.

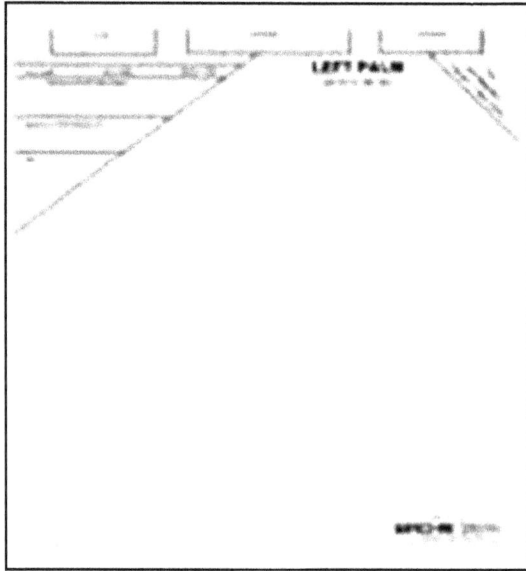

Palm print cards.

Blood, Semen, Urine, Saliva

It is unlikely that you will find semen on an environmental crime scene, but blood, saliva, and even urine may turn up. DNA can be extracted under some circumstances from scenes. Using a Swab safe kit or other accepted kit, use this process:

1. Moisten swab with sterile water
2. Swab fluids
3. Swab area
4. Swab surrounding area for control

These items should never be bagged in plastic, only in paper bags. Plastic traps moisture which can cause mold and mildew. Alternate Light Source (ALS) expresses color wavelengths in nanometers (nM) to allow the technician to find evidence invisible to the eye such as semen, blood, and fibers in difficult cases.

The orange and yellow wavelengths excite chemical stains used after Cyanoacrylate Ester fuming is done. Then the print is photographed at a 1:1 ratio with a camera.

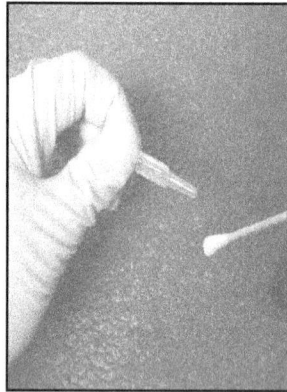

Blood Prints

Prints made by fingers with blood on them are called patent prints. Patent print in blood on tile, stained with Amido Black.

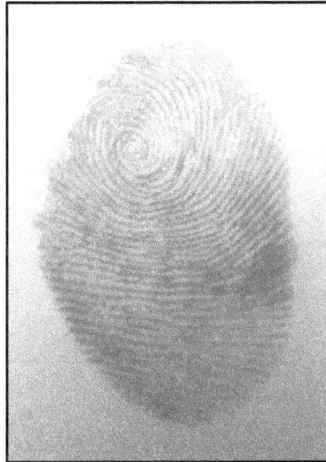

This is a blood print on tile, stained with Amido Black

Patent prints are often made when the straw-colored liquid plasma from blood is transferred to a surface. The red cells stick to the hand or finger, so the print is often hard to see, or invisible. The Amido Black powder is mixed with methanol and acetic acid to make a solution. The Amido Black stains the blood or plasma. Another dye called Coomasie Blue can be used in place of Amido Black.

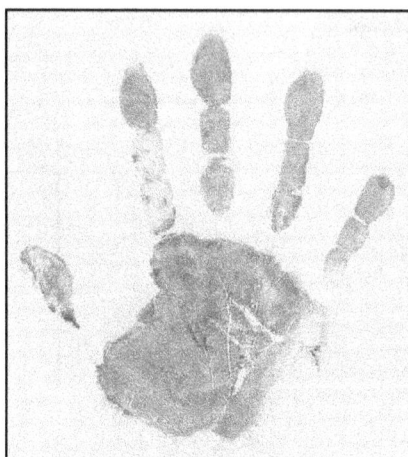

This is a blood print on tile, stained with Coomassie Blue.

Is It Blood?

In order to find out if a fluid is blood, you can use a test for specificity. There are two that are popular: Phenolphthalein, and Leuco-malachite Green.

With Phenolphthalein, blood causes a pink stain in just a few seconds. This test is considered by many field technicians as being one of the most reliable presumptive tests for the presence of blood.

With Leuco-malachite Green, an intense blue/green color reaction in three seconds is presumptive evidence that blood is present. Leuco-malachite Green has long been a favorite of field investigators because of its high sensitivity (1:300,000).

These chemicals are used by blotting the suspected blood with filter paper or paper towels, if filter paper isn't available. The paper is moistened with sterile water before using the chemicals.

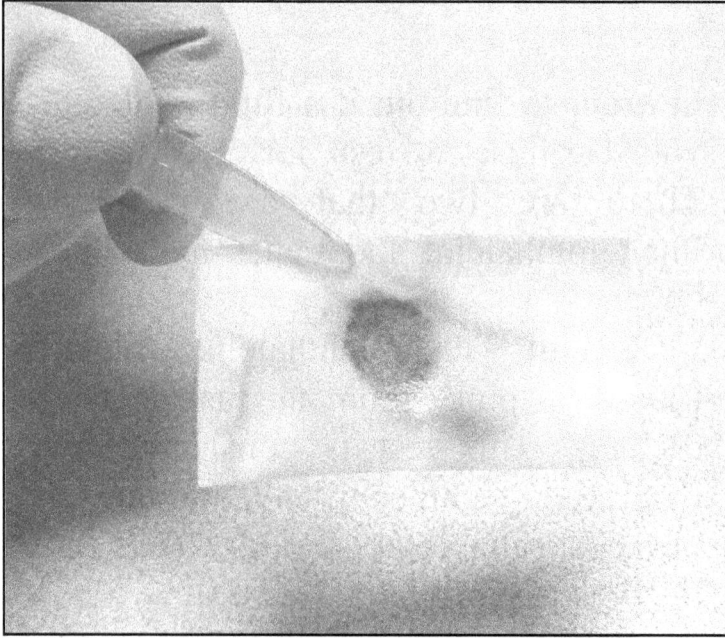

This filter paper has blood on it. Phenolphthalein is reacting to blood.

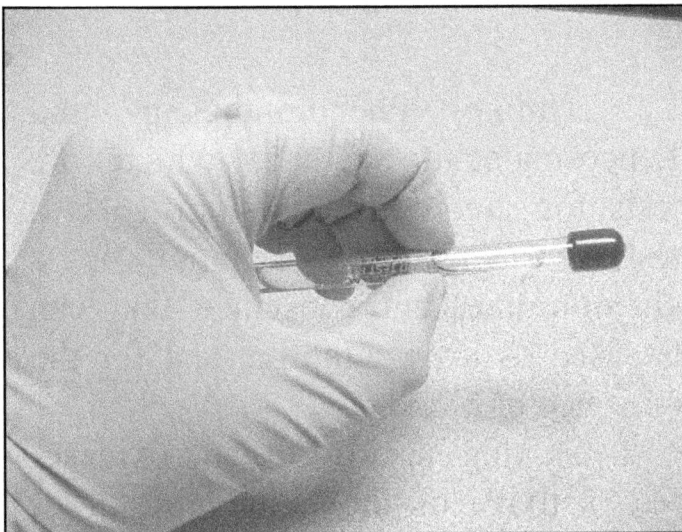

This is a Leuco-malachite Green test.

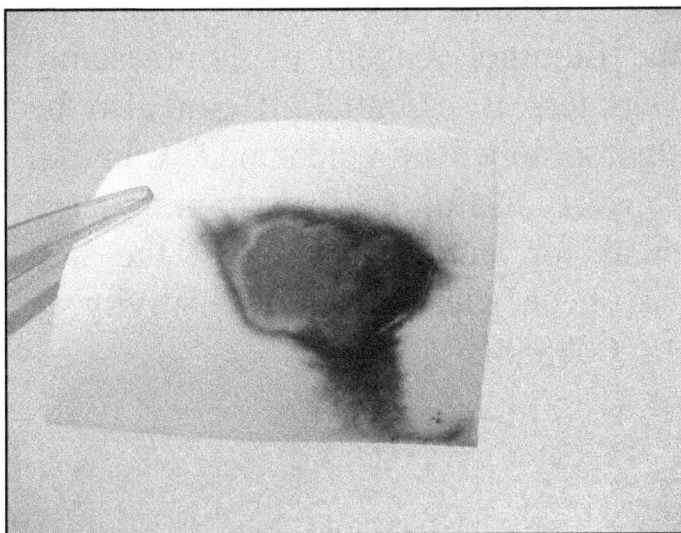

This filter paper has blood on it.
Leuco-malachite Green is reacting to
the blood.

Unlike Phenolphthalein and Leuco-malachite Green, which are tests for specificity, Luminol 16 is a test for sensitivity; Luminol is a chemiluminescent substance that can be used as a presumptive test for the presence of blood.

Making use of the peroxidase-like activity of the heme portion of hemoglobin, Luminol 16 produces a bluishwhite light that can be viewed in total darkness.

Invisible blood stains react with the Luminol reagent by luminescing. Darkness is essential. It can also be Photographed or videotaped. Luminol is a very useful test for searching large areas for blood especially if the area has been cleaned up. Sensitivity is 1:5,000,000.

This carpet has blood prints on it, in daylight. The Luminol is glowing even in daylight. Note the glow-in-the-dark scale.

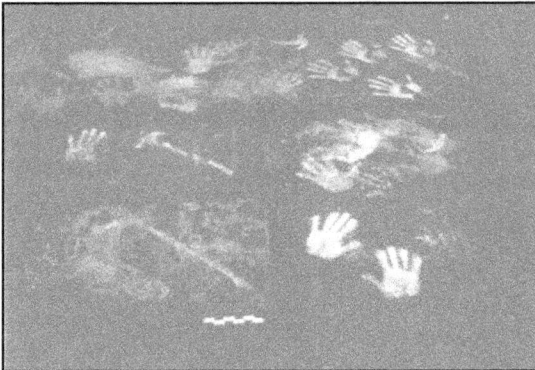

In darkness, the Luminol glows brightly. Note the glow-in-the-dark scale.

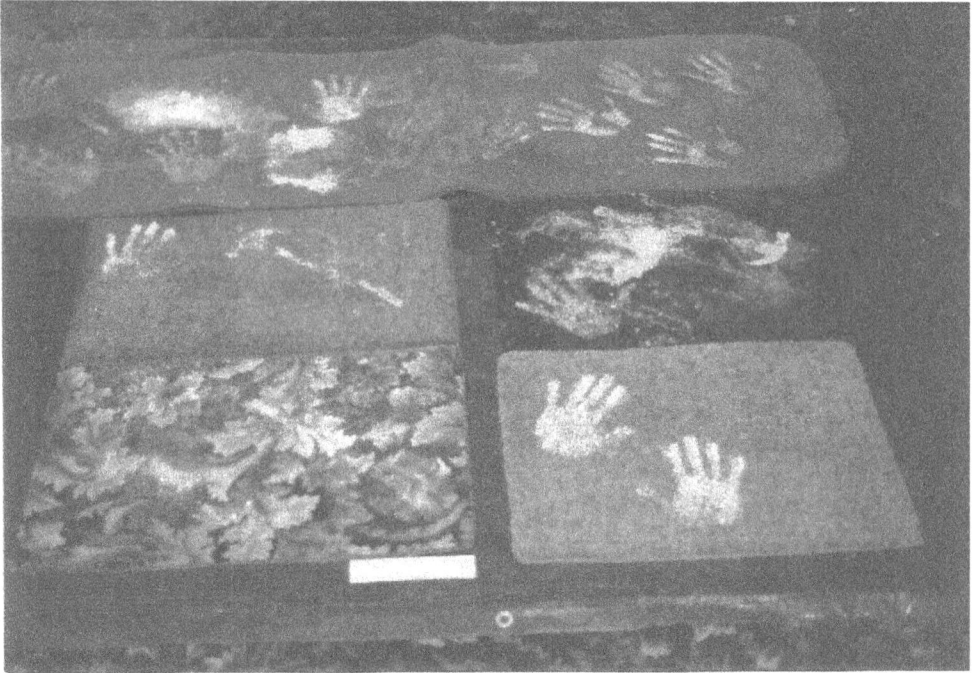

*The same carpet in darkness with
A flashlight used, time exposure
of 90 seconds. The Luminol shows
palms, spatter, and a patent print from
a hammer dipped in blood. Note the
glow-in-the-dark scale.*

Wet Items for Processing

Wet items must be dried properly and thoroughly to avoid mold and fungus. Transport these items in paper bags, and transport to drying cabinet.

Not every agency has a drying cabinet. Most medical examiner's offices have one drying cabinet. Sealing off a room and stringing up a clothesline isn't the best way to do it, but will work in a pinch.

Dry Items for Processing

With dry items, they can generally be stored in paper or plastic. Use the following procedure:

1. Package in plastic bags

2. Seal with Evidence Tape

3. Seal in plastic bags

4. Sign across tape

5. Case number on front in indelible ink

Voir Dire

A defense attorney will try to destroy your credibility in court. Knowing the basics will help you in a process called Voir Dire, which is Latin for *"to seek the truth"* or *"to seek, to say"*, depending on how you translate it.

An example of a Voir Dire question is "What is the name of the science of fingerprinting or fingerprint identification?" The answer of course is "dactyloscopy". If you do not know, the attorney can follow this up by saying "you want to be qualified as an expert, but you do not even know what the name of your own science is called?"

Processing
Contaminated Items

When processing contaminated items for latents, the used dust should not be saved and reused. The brushes, magnetic wands, or whatever, should not be reused. If the item has a toxic chemical or is radioactive, reusing these items can cause health problems for the CSI or other members of the unit.

Improvised Explosive Devices

An IED or Improvised Explosive Device is a device placed or fabricated in an improvised manner incorporating destructive, lethal, noxious, pyrotechnic, or incendiary chemicals and designed to destroy, incapacitate, harass, or distract. It may incorporate military stores, but is normally devised from nonmilitary components.

An explosive is anything that, once ignited, burns extremely rapidly and produces a large amount of hot gas in the process. The hot gas expands very rapidly and applies pressure. Other explosives that you commonly hear about are nitroglycerin and TNT, but anything from gasoline to ammonium nitrate fertilizer to special plastic explosives are in the same class.

These types of explosives can be used to booby trap environmental crime scenes.

Booby Traps

Clandestine meth lab hazards, fires, explosions from unstable chemical processes, booby traps, toxic fumes including invisible poison phosphene gas, and hazardous chemical wastes, including lye, red phosphorus, hydrochloric acid, cyanide, chlorinated solvents, are all dangerous items that can be found on crime scenes.

Sometimes drug dealers will set up bombs, chemical reactors, or booby traps using guns or explosives. Some chemical bombs and reactions can be made using household products such as pool chlorine, turpentine, gasoline, muriatic acid, or brake fluid.

A meth lab is both a hazardous crime scene and an environmental crime scene. Some of the salts used in making methamphetamine are dangerous and explosive. Shock can cause massive explosions.

Boiling Liquid Expanding Vapor Explosion (BLEVE), is the explosion associated with the sudden failure of a container whose contents are a flammable liquefied compressed gas. Typically a BLEVE is due to flame impingement which causes an increased pressure inside the vessel and a weakening of the vessel material. Upon rupture, the pressure inside the vessel is immediately reduced to atmospheric pressure.

At atmospheric pressure, the contents of the vessel instantly boil and vaporize. The vapors of the material occupy several hundred times the space that the liquid had required. This produces a quickly expanding vapor cloud which can be ignited causing a massive explosion and fireball.

A fire at a home depot or a hardware store can result in an environmental hazard of the type that your city or county has never seen. It can be unbelievably dangerous to the rescuers and to the residents in the area. Likewise, a train or truck carrying solids or liquids can cause a massive contamination or explosion.

When these types of hazards are noted, it is important to call out experts. Keep the numbers handy for these experts:

- FBI Field Office

- Local Ofc. Of Emergency Management

- Local Health Department

- DEA Clandestine Lab Team

Making a Fool of Yourself

In one agency, I ran the crime scene unit. I was considered the expert. I did all the training, budgeting, ordering, purchasing, and most of the processing. I was the "go-to guy".

I got a call about a suspicious package. An old looking suitcase was found in a carport at a home. There were oily stains on the outside, and the thing was held together with twine.

I interviewed the homeowner who swore he had never seen it before, and had no idea how it got there. Everything about this screamed "bomb" to me. I called the supervisor and said I wanted to call in the bomb squad from the neighboring department, since we had no bomb squad. The sergeant deferred to my training and experience.

If this were a bomb, I would be a hero. I would have saved this man's house, countless lives, and would have immediately justified the thousands spent on my CSI training. I could just picture the awards, honors, and accolades.

The bomb guy got there, and was so suspicious, he wouldn't risk his dog on this one. A robot was sent in. The robot eventually cut the twine, and the suitcase was opened. Newspapers.

The suitcase contained original copies of the New York Times. The sinking of the Titanic. The murder of JFK. The Beatles arrive in America. The Hindenburg goes down in flames. The death of Adolf Hitler. The Japanese bomb Pearl. Nuclear bombs dropped on Hiroshima. The Giants win the pennant.

Some of the greatest moments in history, from the front page of the greatest paper in America. We read the papers with awe, then the homeowner told us "oh yeah, dad said he was dropping this by".

My awards and accolades were never to be, and the guys on the department made fun of me for months. I did the right thing, and I would do it again.

If that suitcase contained twenty pounds of Semtex, we would have been looking at some dead cops. I would rather be red-faced and not have to go to a bunch of cop funerals, where we had to bury as six foot casket containing a lunch bag full of remains, since that would be all we would have found.

React to your training. Everyone makes a fool of himself sometimes. Imagine how you would feel if you ignored the training and had to go to a few cop funerals because you didn't want to look foolish.

The awards and accolades will come eventually, if you live long enough.

Death Investigation

The cause of death is what killed someone. The manner of death is how it happened. There are 5 manners of death: homicide, accidental, suicide, natural, and undetermined.

There are many manners of death: accidental asphyxia, over medication, industrial, vehicular, leisure related, falls, plant or animal related, drowning, accidental shooting, fires, nature related, impalement, accidental poisoning and many others.

Every death caused by another is a homicide. Some are murder, some are manslaughter, and some are legally justifiable.

Undetermined causes of death were once referred to as GOK, or God Only Knows. Undetermined means we cant be sure, we don't know, we just cant say, because there is not enough evidence. A skeleton found in the water without any stab wounds, gunshots, fractured hyoid bone, or other indicators, may be attributed to drowning due to a lack of other evidence. Not all medical examiners are willing to make this type of ruling.

There are five stages of decomposition: fresh, bloat, decay, dry, and remains. Forensic entomology, the absence or presence of maggots and the life cycle of certain worms and blowflies, can help determine the time of death within a day or two.

Forensic botany, the life cycle of certain plants growing through body parts and skeletal remains, can also determine the time of death within a few days.

The absence or presence of adipocere, the hardening of fat that comes into contact with water can tell us if a body is an old burial or a fresher body dumped in a field or graveyard.

Death investigation is a book in itself. The idea is to relate to you that you must get training and experience to understand what these death scenes mean.

An environmental crime scene that results in human death is a very serious matter.

Final Thoughts

We all have to live on this planet. Without seeming to quote mysticism or new age philosophy, the earth is like our mother, and we must have respect for her.

Allowing other people to do things out of greed or ignorance which kill plants, animals, birds, people, or contaminate water or soil, is just not good policing.

Many police departments will not want to spend time or resources on this type of crime; they will want to spend money on "sexy" crimes, like dealing drugs to children, rape, and murder.

Do the right thing, at the right time, for the right reason, and the truth will always bear you up. Treat these crimes with respect and gravity.

NOTES

_____

_____

_____

_____

_____

_____

_____

_____

_____

_____

_____

_____

_____

_____

_____

_____

_____

_____

_____

_____

_____

_____

_____

NOTES

NOTES

NOTES

WM

WHITE MOUNTAIN PUBLISHING CO.
MIAMI, FLORIDA

ISBN 978-0-9834866-4-0